th

Sounds&Letters 15

T0025472

KNOWLEDGE
BOOKS

think	thumb
three	thong
thick	thin
thirty	

th

think

3

thumb

5

three

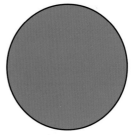

thong

thick _____

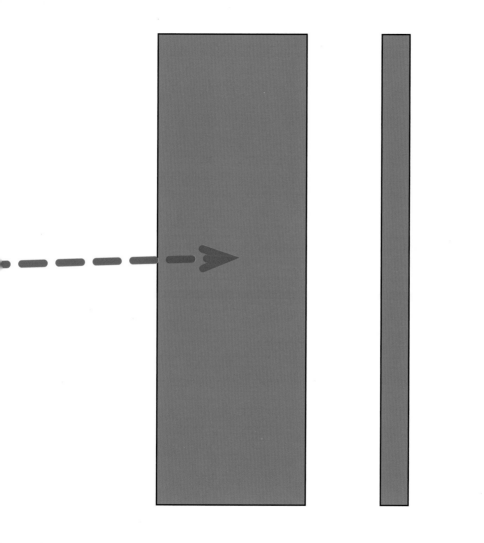

thin

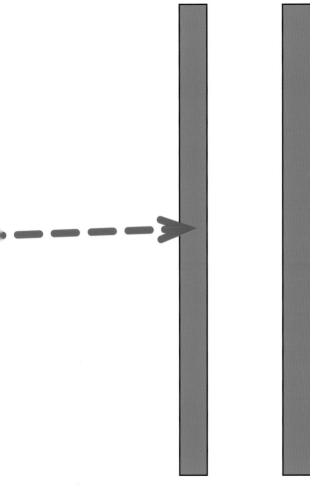

thirty

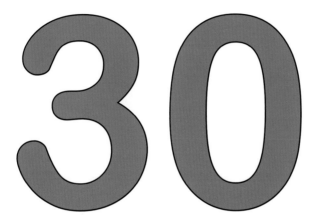

think	thumb
three	thong
thick	thin
thirty	

Knowledge Books and Software
PO Box 50 Sandgate, Queensland 4017 Australia
p. +617-55680288 f. +617-55680277 email: sales@kbs.com.au

First Published 2022
ISBN 9781922516879
Text and editing: Carole Crimeen
Design and layout: Suzanne Fletcher
Publisher: Robert Watts

Series Information: **Sounds and Letters**

Credits
Photographs: Cover © wavebreakmedia; p. 1 © Susan Schmitz, Protasov AN, Sean Locke Photography, gomolach; p. 3 © Brian A Jackson; p. 5 © Vitalinka; p. 9 © Serhii Tsyhanok/ Shutterstock.

Phonic support books are a wonderful resource for emergent readers as they encourage independent reading and help students make the link between letters and the sounds they represent.

Have students identify the images on the title page to listen for the sound that they will hear through the book.

Encourage students to point to each word as they read through the book.

ISBN: 9781922516879

9 781922 516879 >

KNOWLEDGE BOOKS

Sounds & Letters